FAMOUS … ALES

To Robert,

with love from,

Svend-Aage, Sharon, Daniel,
Katrina & Michela

Hans Christian Andersen

FAMOUS FAIRY TALES

Little Claus and Big Claus
The Little Match Girl · It's Quite True!
The Fir Tree

Illustrations by Mads Stage

SESAM

Translation: Jean Hersholt

Cover layout: Sabine Brandt

Typesetting: Christensen Grafisk ApS

Printer: Nørhaven Book, Viborg

Binder: D. L. Cléments Eftf. A/S

ISBN 87-11-13697-9

Contents

Little Claus and Big Claus

In a village there lived two men who had the self-same name. Both were named Claus. But one of them owned four horses, and the other owned only one horse; so to distinguish between them people called the man who had four horses Big Claus, and the man who had only one horse Little Claus. Now I will tell you what happened to these two, for this is a true story.

The whole week through, Little Claus had to plough for Big Claus and lend him his only horse. In return, Big Claus lent him all four of his horses, but only for one day a week and that was Sunday.

Each Sunday how proudly Little Claus cracked his whip over all the five horses, which were as good as his own on that day. How brightly the sun shone. How merry were the church bells that rang in the steeple. How well dressed were all the people who passed him with hymn books tucked under their arms. And as they went their way to church, to hear the parson preach, how the people did stare to see Little Claus ploughing with all five horses. This made him feel so proud that he would crack his whip and holler, "Gee up, all my horses."

"You must not say that," Big Claus told him. "You know as well as I do that only one of those horses is yours." But no sooner did another bevy of churchgoers come by than Little Claus forgot he must not say it, and hollered, "Gee up, all my horses."

"Don't you say that again," Big Claus told him. "If you do, I'll knock your horse down dead in his traces, and that will be the end of him."

"You won't catch me saying it again," Little Claus promised. But as soon as people came by, nodding to him and wishing him "Good morning," he was so pleased and so proud of how grand it looked to have five horses ploughing his field, that he hollered again, "Gee up, all my horses!"

"I'll Gee up your horses for you," Big Claus said, and he snatched up a tethering mallet, and he knocked Little Claus's one and only horse on the head so hard that it fell down dead.

"Now I haven't any horse at all," said Little Claus, and he began to cry. But by and by he skinned his dead horse and hung the hide to dry in the wind. Then he crammed the dry skin in a sack, slung it up over his shoulder, and set out to sell it in the nearest town.

It was a long way to go, and he had to pass through a dark, dismal forest. Suddenly a terrible storm came up, and he lost his way. Before he could find it again, evening overtook him. The town was still a long way off, and he had come too far to get back home before night.

Not far from the road he saw a large farmhouse. The shutters were closed, but light showed through a crack at the top of the windows. "Maybe they'll let me spend the night

here," Little Claus thought, as he went to the door and knocked.

The farmer's wife opened it, but when she heard what he wanted she told him to go away. She said her husband was not home, and she would not have any strangers in the house.

"Then I'll have to sleep outside," Little Claus decided, as she slammed the door in his face.

Near the farmhouse stood a large haystack, leading up to the thatched roof of a shed which lay between it and the house. "That's where I'll sleep," said Little Claus when he noticed the thatch. "It will make a wonderful bed. All I hope is that the stork doesn't fly down and bite my legs." For a stork was actually standing guard on the roof where it had a nest.

So Little Claus climbed to the roof of the shed. As he turned over to make himself comfortable, he discovered that the farmhouse shutters did not come quite to the top of the windows, and he could see over them. He could see into a room where a big table was spread with wine and roast meat and a delicious fish. The farmer's wife and the sexton were sitting there at the table, all by themselves. She kept helping him to wine, and he kept helping himself to fish. He must have loved fish.

"Oh, if only I could have some too," thought Little Claus. By craning his neck toward the window he caught sight of a great, appetizing cake. Why, they were feasting in there!

Just then he heard someone riding down the road to the house. It was the farmer coming home. He was an excellent man except for just one thing. He could not stand the sight of a sexton. If he so much as caught a glimpse of one, he would fly into a furious rage, which was the reason why the sexton had gone to see the farmer's wife while her husband was away from home, and the good woman could do no less than set before him all the good things to eat that she had in the house. When she heard the farmer coming, she trembled for the sexton, and begged him to creep into a big empty chest which stood in one corner of the room. He lost no time about it, because he knew full well that her poor husband could not stand the sight of a sexton. The woman quickly set aside the wine and hid the good food in her oven, because if her husband had seen the feast he would have asked questions hard to answer.

"Oh, dear!" Up on the shed Little Claus sighed to see all the good food disappearing.

"Who's up there?" the farmer peered at Little Claus. "Whatever are you doing up there? Come into the house with me." So Little Claus came down. He told the farmer how he had lost his way, and asked if he could have shelter for the night.

"Of course," said the farmer, "but first let's have something to eat."

The farmer's wife received them well, laid the whole table, and set before them a big bowl of porridge. The farmer was hungry and ate it with a good appetite, but Little Claus was thinking about the good roast meat, that fish and that cake in the oven. Beside his feet under the table lay his sack with the horsehide, for as we know he was on his way to sell it in the town. Not liking the porridge at all, Little Claus trod on the sack, and the dry hide gave a loud squeak.

"Sh!" Little Claus said to his sack, at the same time that he trod on it so hard that it squeaked even louder.

"What on earth have you got in there?" said the farmer.

"Oh, just a conjuror," said Little Claus. "He tells me we don't have to eat porridge, because he has conjured up a whole oven-full of roast meat, fish, and cake for us."

"What do you say?" said the farmer. He made haste to open the oven, where he found all the good dishes. His wife had hidden them there, but he quite believed that they had been conjured up by the wizard in the sack. His wife did not dare open her mouth as she helped them to their fill of meat, fish and cake.

Then Little Claus trod upon the sack to make it squeak again.

"What does he say now?" asked the farmer.

"He says," Little Claus answered, "that there are three bottles of wine for us in the corner by the oven."

So the woman had to bring out the wine she had hidden. The farmer drank it till he grew merry, and wanted to get himself a conjuror just like the one Little Claus carried in his sack.

"Can he conjure up the devil?" the farmer wondered. "I'm in just the mood to meet him."

"Oh, yes," said Little Claus. "My conjuror can do anything I tell him. Can't you?" he asked and trod upon the sack till it squeaked. "Did you hear him answer? He said 'Yes.' He can conjure up the devil, but he's afraid we won't like the look of him."

"Oh, I'm not afraid. What's he like?"

"Well, he looks an awful lot like a sexton."

"Ho," said the farmer, "as ugly as that? I can't bear the sight of a sexton. But don't let that stop us. Now that I know it's just the devil I shan't mind it so much. I'll face him, provided he doesn't come near me."

"Wait, while I talk with my conjuror." Little Claus trod on the sack and stooped down to listen.

"What does he say?"

"He says for you to go and open that big chest in the corner, and there you'll find the devil doubled up inside it. But you must hold fast to the lid, so he doesn't pop out."

"Will you help me hold it?" said the farmer. He went to the chest in which his wife bad hidden the sexton – once frightened, now terrified. The farmer lifted the lid a little, and peeped in.

"Ho!" he sprang back, "I saw him, and he's the image of our sexton, a horrible sight!" After that they needed another drink, and sat there drinking far into the night.

"You must sell me your conjuror," said the farmer. "You

can fix your own price. I'd pay you a bushel of money right away."

"Oh, I couldn't do that," Little Claus said. "Just think how useful my conjuror is."

"But I'd so like to have him." The farmer kept begging to buy it.

"Well," said Little Claus at last, "you've been kind enough to give me a night's lodging, so I can't say no. You shall have my sack for a bushel of money, but it must be full to the brim."

"You shall have it," said the farmer. "But you must take that chest along with you too. I won't have it in the house another hour. He might still be inside it. You never can tell."

So Little Claus sold his sack with the dried horsehide in it, and was paid a bushel of money, measured up to the brim. The farmer gave him a wheelbarrow too, in which to wheel away the money and the chest.

"Fare you well," said Little Claus, and on he went with his money and his chest with the sexton in it. On the further side of the forest was a deep, wide river, where the current ran so strong that it was almost impossible to swim against it. A big new bridge had been built across the river, and when Little Claus came to the middle of it he said, very loud so the sexton could hear him:

"Now what would I be doing with this silly chest? It's as heavy as stone, and I'm too tired to wheel it any further. So I'll throw it in the river, and if it drifts down to my house, well and good, but if it sinks I haven't lost much." Then he tilted the chest a little, as if he were about to tip it into the river.

"Stop! Don't!" the sexton shouted inside. "Let me get out first."

"Oh," said Little Claus pretending to be frightened, "is he still there? Then I'd better throw him into the river and drown him."

"Oh no, don't do that to me!" the sexton shouted. "I'd give a bushel of money to get out of this."

"Why, that's altogether different," said Little Claus, opening the chest. The sexton popped out at once, pushed the empty chest into the water and hurried home to give Little Claus a bushel of money. What with the farmer's bushel and the sexton's bushel, Little Claus had his wheelbarrow quite full.

"I got a good price for my horse," he said when he got home and emptied all the money in a heap on the floor of his room. "How Big Claus will fret when he finds out that my one horse has made me so rich, but I won't tell him how I managed it." Then he sent a boy to borrow a bushel measure from Big Claus.

"Whatever would he want with it?" Big Claus wondered, and smeared pitch on the bottom of the bushel so that a little of what he measured would stick to it. And so it happened that when he got his measure back he found three newly minted pieces of silver stuck to it.

"What's this?" Big Claus ran to see Little Claus. "Where did you get so much money?"

"Oh, that's what I got for the horsehide I sold last night."

"Heavens above! How the price of hides must have gone up." Big Claus ran home, took an axe and knocked all four of his horses on the head. Then be ripped their hides off, and set out to town with them.

"Hides, hides! Who'll buy hides?" he bawled, up and down the streets. All the shoemakers and tanners came running to ask what their price was. "A bushel of money apiece," he told them.

"Are you crazy?" they asked. "Do you think we spend money by the bushel?"

"Hides, hides! Who'll buy hides?" he kept on shouting, and to those who asked how much, he said, "A bushel of money."

"He takes us for fools," they said. The shoemakers took their straps, and the tanners their leather aprons, and they beat Big Claus through the town.

"Hides, hides!" they mocked him. "We'll tan your hide for you if you don't get out of town." Big Claus had to run as fast as he could. He had never been beaten so badly.

"Little Claus will pay for this," he said when he got back home. "I'll kill him for it."

Now it so happened that Little Claus's old grandmother had just died. She had been as cross as could be – never a kind word did she have for him – but he was sorry to see her die. He put the dead woman in his own warm bed, just in case she came to life again, and let her lie there all night while he took a nap in a chair in the corner, as he had done so often before.

As be sat there in the night, the door opened and in came Big Claus with an axe. He knew exactly where Little Claus's bed was, so he went straight to it and knocked the dead grandmother on the head, under the impression that she was Little Claus.

"There," he said, "you won't fool me again." Then he went home.

"What a wicked man," said Little Claus. "Why, he would have killed me. It's lucky for my grandmother that she was already dead, or he'd have been the death of her."

He dressed up his old grandmother in her Sunday best, borrowed a neighbor's horse, and hitched up his cart. On the back seat he propped up his grandmother, wedged in so that the jolts would not topple her over, and away they went through the forest.

When the sun came up they drew abreast of a large inn, where Little Claus halted and went in to get himself some breakfast. The innkeeper was a wealthy man, and a good enough fellow in his way, but his temper was as fiery as if he were made of pepper and snuff.

"Good morning," he said to Little Claus. "You're up and dressed mighty early."

"Yes," said Little Claus. "I am bound for the town with my old grandmother, who is sitting out there in the cart. I can't get her to come in, but you might take her a glass of mead. You'll have to shout to make her hear you, for she's deaf as a post."

"I'll take it right out." The innkeeper poured a glass full of mead and took it to the dead grandmother, who sat stiffly in the cart.

"Your grandson sent you a glass of mead," said the innkeeper, but the dead woman said never a word. She just sat there.

"Don't you hear me?" the innkeeper shouted his loudest. "Here's a glass of mead from your grandson."

Time after time he shouted it, but she did not budge. He flew into such a rage that he threw the glass in her face. The mead splashed all over her as she fell over backward, for she was just propped up, not tied in place.

"Confound it!" Little Claus rushed out the door and took the innkeeper by the throat. "You've gone and killed my grandmother. Look! There's a big hole in her forehead."

"Oh, what a calamity!" The innkeeper wrung his hands. "And all because of my fiery temper. Dear Little Claus, I'll give you a bushel of money, and I'll bury your grandmother as if she were my very own. But you must hush this thing up for me, or they'll chop off my head – how I'd hate it."

So it came about that Little Claus got another bushel of money, and the landlord buried the old grandmother as if she had been his own.

Just as soon as Little Claus got home, he sent a boy to borrow a bushel measure from Big Claus.

"Little Claus wants to borrow it?" Big Claus asked. "Didn't I kill him? I'll go and see about that." So he himself took the measure over to Little Claus.

"Where did you get all that money?" he asked when he saw the height of the money pile.

"When you killed my grandmother instead of me," Little Claus told him, "I sold her for a bushel of money."

"Heavens above! That was indeed a good price," said Big Claus. He hurried home, took an axe, and knocked his old grandmother on the head. Then he put her in a cart, drove off to town, and asked the apothecary if he wanted to buy a dead body.

"Whose dead body?" asked the apothecary. "Where'd you get it?"

"It's my grandmother's dead body. I killed her for a bushel of money," Big Claus told him.

"Lord," said the apothecary. "Man, you must be crazy. Don't talk like that or they'll chop off your head." Then he told him straight he had done a wicked deed, that he was a terrible fellow, and that the worst of punishments was much too good for him. Big Claus got frightened. He jumped in his cart, whipped up the horses, and drove home as fast as they would take him. The apothecary and everyone else thought he must be a madman, so they did not stand in his way.

"I'll see that you pay for this," said Big Claus when he reached the highroad. "Oh, won't I make you pay for this, Little Claus!" The moment he got home he took the biggest sack he could find, went to see Little Claus, and said:

"You've deceived me again. First I killed my four horses. Then I killed my old grandmother, and it's all your fault. But I'll make sure you don't make a fool of me again." Then he caught Little Claus and put him in the sack, slung it up over his back and told him, "Now I shall take you and drown you."

It was a long way to the river, and Little Claus was no light load. The road went by the church, and as they passed they could hear the organ playing and the people singing very beautifully. Big Claus set down his sack just outside the church door. He thought the best thing for him to do was to go in to hear a hymn before he went any further. Little Claus was securely tied in the sack, and all the people were inside the church. So Big Claus went in too.

"Oh dear, oh dear!" Little Claus sighed in the sack. Twist and turn as he might, he could not untie the knot. Then a white-haired old cattle drover came by, leaning heavily on his staff. The herd of bulls and cows he was driving bumped against the sack Little Claus was in, and overturned it.

"Oh dear," Little Claus sighed. "I'm so young to be going to Heaven."

"While I," said the cattle drover, "am too old for this earth, yet Heaven will not send for me."

"Open the sack!" Little Claus shouted. "Get in and take my place. You'll go straight to Heaven."

"That's where I want to be," said the drover, as he undid the sack. Little Claus jumped out at once. "You must look after my cattle," the old man said as he crawled in. As soon as Little Claus fastened the sack, he walked away from there with all the bulls and cows.

Presently Big Claus came out of church. He took the sack on his back and found it light, for the old drover was no more than half as heavy as Little Claus.

"How light my burden is, all because I've been listening to a hymn," said Big Claus. He went on to the deep wide river, and threw the sack with the old cattle drover into the water.

"You'll never trick me again," Big Claus said, for he thought he had seen the last splash of Little Claus.

He started home, but when he came to the crossroads he met Little Claus and all his cattle.

"Where did you come from?" Big Claus exclaimed. "Didn't I just drown you?"

"Yes," said Little Claus. "You threw me in the river half an hour ago."

"Then how did you come by such a fine herd of cattle?" Big Claus wanted to know.

"Oh, they're sea cattle," said Little Claus. "I'll tell you how I got them, because I'm obliged to you for drowning me. I'm a made man now. I can't begin to tell you how rich I am."

"But when I was in the sack, with the wind whistling in my ears as you dropped me off the bridge into the cold water, I was frightened enough. I went straight to the bottom, but it didn't hurt me because of all the fine soft grass down there. Someone opened the sack, and a beautiful maiden took my hand. Her clothes were white as snow, and she had a green wreath in her floating hair. She said, 'So you've come, Little Claus. Here's a herd of cattle for you, but they are just the beginning of my presents. A mile further up the road another herd awaits you.'

"Then I saw that the river is a great highway for the

people who live in the sea. Down on the bottom of the river they walked and drove their cattle straight in from the sea to the land where the rivers end. The flowers down there are fragrant. The grass is fresh, and fish flit by as birds do up here. The people are fine, and so are the cattle that come grazing along the roadside."

"Then why are you back so soon?" Big Claus asked. "If it's all so beautiful, I'd have stayed there."

"Well," said Little Claus, "I'm being particularly sly. You remember I said the sea maiden told me to go one mile up the road and I'd find another herd of cattle. By 'road' she meant the river, for that's the only way she travels. But I know how the river turns and twists, and it seemed too roundabout a way of getting there. By coming up on land I took a short cut that saves me half a mile. So I get my cattle that much sooner."

"You are a lucky man," said Big Claus. "Do you think I would get me some cattle too if I went down to the bottom of the river?"

"Oh, I'm sure you would," said Little Claus. "Don't expect me to carry you there in a sack, because you're too heavy for me, but if you walk to the river and crawl into the sack, I'll throw you in with the greatest of pleasure."

"Thank you," said Big Claus, "but remember, if I don't get a herd of sea cattle down there, I'll give you a thrashing, believe me."

"Would you really?" said Little Claus.

As they came to the river, the thirsty cattle saw the water

and rushed to drink it. Little Claus said, "See what a hurry they are in to get back to the bottom of the river."

"Help me get there first," Big Claus commanded, "or I'll give you that beating right now." He struggled into the big sack, which had been lying across the back of one of the cattle. "Put a stone in, or I'm afraid I shan't sink," said Big Claus.

"No fear of that," said Little Claus, but he put a big stone in the sack, tied it tightly, and pushed it into the river. Splash! Up flew the water and down to the bottom sank Big Claus.

"I'm afraid he won't find what I found!" said Little Claus, as he herded all his cattle home.

The Little Match Girl

It was so terribly cold. Snow was falling, and it was almost dark. Evening came on, the last evening of the year. In the cold and gloom a poor little girl, bareheaded and barefoot, was walking through the streets. Of course when she had

left her house she had been wearing slippers, but what good had they been? They were very big slippers, way too big for her, for they belonged to her mother. The little girl had lost them running across the road, where two carriages had rattled by terribly fast. One slipper she had not been able to find again, and a boy had run off with the other, saying he could use it very well as a cradle some day when he had children of his own. And so the little girl walked on her naked feet, which were quite red and blue with the cold. In an old apron she carried several packages of matches, and she held a box of them in her hand. No one had bought any from her all day long, and no one had given her a penny.

Shivering with cold and hunger, she crept along, a picture of misery, poor little girl! The snowflakes fell on her long fair hair, which hung in pretty curls over her neck. But she did not think of her pretty curls now. In all the windows lights were shining, and there was a wonderful smell of roast goose, for it was New Year's Eve. Yes, she thought of that!

In a corner formed by two houses, one of which projected farther out into the street than the other, she sat down and drew up her little feet under her. She was getting colder and colder, but did not dare to go home, for she had sold no matches, nor earned a single penny, and her father would surely beat her. Besides, it was cold at home, for they had nothing over them but a roof through which the wind whistled even though the biggest cracks had been stuffed with straw and rags.

Her hands were almost dead with cold. Oh, how much one little match might warm her! If she could only take one

from the box and rub it against the wall and warm her hands. She drew one out. R-r-ratch! How it sputtered and burned! It made a warm, bright flame, like a little candle, as she held her hands over it; but it gave a strange light! It really seemed to the little girl as if she were sitting before a great iron stove with shiny brass knobs and a brass cover. How wonderfully the fire burned! How comfortable it was! The youngster stretched out her feet to warm them too; then the little flame went out, the stove vanished, and she had only the remains of the burnt match in her hand.

She struck another match against the wall. It burned brightly, and when the light fell upon the wall it became transparent like a thin veil, and she could see through it into a room. On the table a snow-white cloth was spread, and on it stood the finest china. The roast goose steamed gloriously, stuffed with apples and prunes. And what was still better, the goose jumped down from the dish and waddled along the floor, with a knife and fork in its breast, right over to the little girl. Then the match went out, and she could see only the thick, cold wall. She lighted another match. Then she was sitting under the most beautiful Christmas tree. It was much larger and much more beautiful than the one she had seen last Christmas through the glass door at the rich merchant's home. Thousands of candles burned on the green branches, and coloured pictures like those in the printshops looked down at her. The little girl reached both her hands toward them. Then the match went out. But the Christmas lights mounted higher. She saw them now as bright stars in the sky. One of them fell down, forming a long line of fire.

"Now someone is dying," thought the little girl, for her old grandmother, the only person who had loved her, and who was now dead, had told her that when a star fell down a soul went up to God.

She rubbed another match against the wall. It became bright again, and in the glow the old grandmother stood clear and shining, kind and lovely.

"Grandmother!" cried the child. "Oh, take me with you! I know you will disappear when the match burns out. You will vanish like the warm stove, the wonderful roast goose and the beautiful big Christmas tree!"

And she quickly struck the whole bundle of matches, for she wished to keep her grandmother with her. And the matches burned with such a glow that it became brighter than daylight. Grandmother had never been so grand and beautiful. She took the little girl in her arms, and both of them flew in brightness and joy above the earth, very, very high, and up there was neither cold, nor hunger, nor fear – they were with God.

But in the corner, leaning against the wall, sat the little girl with red cheeks and a smile on her face, frozen to death on the last evening of the old year. The New Year's sun rose upon the little dead body. The child sat there, stiff and cold, holding the matches, of which one bundle was almost burned.

"She wanted to warm herself," the people said. No one imagined what beautiful things she had seen, and how happily she had gone with her old grandmother into the bright New Year.

It's Quite True!

"It's a dreadful story!" said a hen, and she said it in a part of town, too, where it had not taken place. "It's a dreadful story to happen in a henhouse. I'm afraid to sleep alone to-night; it's a good thing, there are many of us on the perch!" And then she told a story that made the feathers of the other hens stand on end and the rooster's comb fall. It's quite true!

But we will begin at the beginning and tell what had happened in a henhouse at the other end of town.

The sun went down, and the hens flew up. One of them was a white-feathered and short-limbed hen who laid her eggs according to the regulations and who was a respectable hen in every way. As she settled herself on the perch, she plucked herself with her beak, and a tiny feather came out.

"There it goes," she said. "No doubt the more I pluck, the more beautiful I will get." But she said it only in fun, for she was considered the jolliest among the hens, although, as we've said before, most respectable. Then she fell asleep.

There was darkness all around, and the hens sat closely together. But the hen that sat closest to the white hen was not asleep; she had heard and had not heard, as one should do in this world, if one wishes to live in peace. But still she could not resist telling it to her nearest neighbour.

"Did you hear what was said? Well, I don't want to mention any names, but there is a hen here who intends to pluck out all her feathers just to make herself look well. If I were a rooster, I would despise her."

Right above the hens lived a mother owl with a father owl and all her little owls. They had sharp ears in that family, and they all heard every word that their neighbour hen had said. They all rolled their eyes, and the mother owl flapped her wings and said; "Don't listen to it. But I suppose you all heard what was said. I heard it with my own ears, and one

must hear a great deal before they fall off. One of the hens has so completely forgotten what is becoming conduct to a hen that she plucks out all her feathers, while the rooster watches her."

"Little pitchers have big ears," said the father owl. "Children shouldn't hear such talk."

"I must tell it to the owl across the road," said the mother owl. "She is such a respectable owl!" And away flew Mamma.

"Hoo-whoo! Hoo-whoo!" they both hooted to the pigeons in the pigeon house across the road. "Have you heard it? Have you heard it? Hoo-whoo! There is a hen who has plucked out all her feathers just to please the rooster. She must be freezing to death; that is, if she isn't dead already. Hoo-whoo! Hoo-whoo!"

"Where? Where?" cooed the pigeons.

"In the yard across the way. I have as good as seen it myself. It is almost not a proper story to tell, but it's quite true!"

"True, true, every word of it," said the pigeons, and cooed down into their poultry yard. "There is a hen, and some say there are two hens, who have plucked out all their feathers in order to look different from the rest and to attract the attention of the rooster."

"Wake up! Wake up!" crowed the rooster, and flew up on the fence. He was still half asleep, but he crowed just the same. "Three hens have died of a broken heart, all for the sake of a rooster, and they have plucked all their feathers out! It's a dreadful story, but I will not keep it to myself. Tell it everywhere!"

"Tell it everywhere!" shrieked the bats; and the hens clucked and the roosters crowed. "Tell it everywhere!"

And so the story traveled from henhouse to henhouse until at last it was carried back to the very same place from where it had really started.

"There are five hens," now ran the tale, "who all have plucked out all their feathers to show which of them had lost the most weight through unhappy love for their rooster. And then they pecked at each other till they bled and all five dropped dead, to the shame and disgrace of their families, and to the great loss of their owner."

And the hen who had lost the little loose feather naturally did not recognize her own story; and as she was a respectable hen, she said, »I despise such hens, but there are many of that kind! Such stories should not be hushed up, and I'll do my best to get the story into the newspapers. Then it will be known all over the country; that will serve those hens right, and their families, too." And it got to the newspapers, and it was printed. And it is quite true. One little feather may grow till it becomes five hens.

The Fir Tree

Out in the woods stood such a pretty little fir tree. It grew in a good place, where it had plenty of sun and plenty of fresh air. Around it stood many tall comrades, both fir trees and pines.

The little fir tree was in a headlong hurry to grow tip. It didn't care a thing for the warm sunshine, or the fresh air, and it took no interest in the peasant children who ran about chattering when they came to pick strawberries or raspberries. Often when the children had picked their pails full, or had gathered long strings of berries threaded on straws, they would sit down to rest near the little fir. "Oh, isn't it a nice little tree?" they would say, "It's the baby of the woods." The little tree did not like their remarks at all.

Next year it shot up a long joint of new growth, and the following year another joint, still longer. You can always tell how old a fir tree is by counting the number of joints it has.

"I wish I were a grown-up tree, like my comrades," the little tree sighed. "Then I could stretch out my branches and see from my top what the world is like. The birds would make me their nesting place, and when the wind blew I could bow back and forth With all the great trees."

It took no pleasure in the sunshine, nor in the birds. The glowing clouds, that sailed overhead at sunrise and sunset, meant nothing to it.

In winter, when the snow lay sparkling on the ground, a hare would often come hopping along and jump right over the little tree. Oh, how irritating that was! That happened for two winters, but when the third winter came the tree was so tall that the hare had to turn aside and hop around it.

"Oh, to grow, grow! To get older and taller," the little tree thought. "That is the most wonderful thing in this world."

In the autumn, woodcutters came and cut down a few of the largest trees. This happened every year. The young fir was no longer a baby tree, and it trembled to see how those stately great trees crashed to the ground, how their limbs were lopped off, and how lean they looked as the naked trunks were loaded onto carts. It could hardly recognize the trees it had known, when the horses pulled them out of the woods.

Where were they going? What would become of them?

In the springtime, when swallows and storks came back, the tree asked them, "Do you know where the other trees went? Have you met them?"

The swallows knew nothing about it, but the stork looked thoughtful and nodded his head. "Yes, I think I met them," he said. "On my way from Egypt I met many new ships, and some had tall, stately masts. They may well have been the trees you mean, for I remember the smell of fir. They were stately and wanted to be remembered to you."

"Oh, I wish I were old enough to travel on the sea. Please tell me what it really is, and how it looks."

"That would take too long to tell," said the stork, and off he strode.

"Rejoice in your youth," said the sunbeams. "Take pride in your growing strength and in the stir of life within you."

And the wind kissed the tree, and the dew wept over it, for the tree was young and without understanding.

When Christmas came near, many young trees were cut down. Some were not even as old or as tall as this fir tree of ours, who was in such a hurry and eager to go travelling. These young trees, which were always the handsomest ones, had their branches left on them when they were loaded on carts and the horses drew them out of the woods.

"Where can they be going?" the fir tree wondered. "They are no taller than I am. One was really much smaller than I am. And why are they allowed to keep all their branches? Where can they be going?"

"We know! We know!" the sparrows chirped. "We have been to town and peeped through the windows. We know where they are going. The greatest splendour and glory you can imagine awaits them. We've peeped through windows. We've seen them planted right in the middle of a warm room, and decked out with the most splendid things – gold apples, good gingerbread, gay toys, and many hundreds of candles."

"And then?" asked the fir tree, trembling in every twig. "And then? What happens then?"

"We saw nothing more. And never have we seen anything that could match it."

"I wonder if I was created for such a glorious future?" The fir tree rejoiced. "Why, that is better than to cross the sea. I'm tormented with longing. Oh, if Christmas would only come! I'm just as tall and grown-up as the trees they chose last year. How I wish I were already in the cart, on my way to the warm room where there's so much splendour and glory.

Then – then something even better, something still more important is bound to happen, or why should they deck me so fine? Yes, there must be something still grander! But what? Oh, how I suffer, and how I long: I don't know what's the matter with me."

"Enjoy us while you may," the air and sunlight told him. "Rejoice in the days of your youth, out here in the open."

But the tree did not rejoice at all. It just grew. It grew and was green both winter and summer – dark evergreen. People who passed it said, "There's a beautiful tree!" And when Christmas time came again they cut it down first. The axe struck deep into its marrow. The tree sighed as it fell to the ground. It felt faint with pain. Instead of the happiness it had expected, the tree was sorry to leave the home where it had grown up. It knew that never again would it see its dear old comrades, the little bushes and the flowers about it – and perhaps not even the birds. The departure was anything but pleasant.

The tree did not get over it until all the trees were unloaded in the yard, and it heard a man say, "That's a splendid one. That's the tree for us." Then came two servants in fine livery, and carried the fir tree into a big splendid drawing-room. Portraits were hung all around the walls. On either side of the white porcelain stove stood great Chinese vases, with lions on the lids of them. There were easy chairs, silkcovered sofas and long tables strewn with picture books, and with toys that were worth a mint of money, or so the children said.

The fir tree was planted in a large tub filled with sand, but no one could see that it was a tub, because it was wrapped in a gay green cloth and set on a many-coloured carpet. How the tree quivered! What would come next? The servants and even the young ladies helped it on with its fine decorations. From its branches they hung little nets cut out of coloured pa-

per, and each net was filled with sweets. Gilded apples and walnuts hung in clusters as if they grew there, and a hundred little white, blue, and even red, candles were fastened to its twigs. Among its green branches swaved dolls that it took to be real living people, for the tree had never seen their like before. And up at its very top was set a large gold tinsel star. It was splendid, I tell you, splendid beyond all words!

"Tonight," they all said, "ah, tonight how the tree will shine!"

"Oh," thought the tree, "if tonight would only come! If only the candles were lit! And after that, what happens then? Will the trees come trooping out of the woods to see me? Will the sparrows flock to the windows? Shall I take root here, and stand in fine ornaments all winter and summer long?"

That was how much it knew about it. All its longing had gone to its bark and set it to aching, which is as bad for a tree as a headache is for us.

Now the candles were lighted. What dazzling splendour! What a blaze of light! The tree quivered so in every bough that a candle set one of its twigs ablaze. It hurt terribly.

"Mercy me!" cried every young lady, and the fire was quickly put out. The tree no longer dared rustle a twig – it was awful! Wouldn't it be terrible if it were to drop one of its ornaments? Its own brilliance dazzled it.

Suddenly the folding doors were thrown back, and a whole flock of children burst in as if they would overturn the tree completely. Their elders marched in after them, more sedately. For a moment, but only for a moment, the young ones were stricken speechless. Then they shouted till the rafters rang. They danced about the tree and plucked off one present after another.

"What are they up to?" the tree wondered. "What will happen next?"

As the candles burned down to the bark they were snuffed out, one by one, and then the children had permission to plunder the tree. They went about it in such earnest that the branches crackled and, if the tree had not been tied to the ceiling by the gold star at the top, it would have tumbled headlong.

The children danced about with their splendid playthings. No one looked at the tree now, except the old nanny who peered in among the branches, but this was only to make sure that not an apple or fig had been overlooked.

"Tell us a story! Tell us a story!" the children clamoured, as they towed a fat little man to the tree. He sat down beneath it and said, "Here we are in the woods, and it will do the tree a lot of good to listen to our story. Mind you, I'll tell only one. Which will you have, the story of Ivedy-Avedy, or the one about Humpty-Dumpty who tumbled downstairs, yet ascended the throne and married the Princess?"

"Ivedy-Avedy," cried some. "Humpty-Dumpty," cried the others. And there was a great hullabaloo. Only, the fir tree held its peace, though it thought to itself, "Am I to be left out of this? Isn't there anything I can do?" For all the fun of the evening had centered upon it, and it had played its part well.

The fat little man told them all about Humpty-Dumpty, who tumbled downstairs, yet ascended the throne and married the Princess. And the children clapped and shouted, "Tell us another one! Tell us another one!" For they wanted to hear about Ivedy-Avedy too, but after Humpty-Dumpty the story telling stopped. The fir tree stood very still as it pondered how the birds in the woods had never told it a story to equal this.

"Humpty-Dumpty tumbled downstairs, yet he married the Princess. Imagine! That must be how things happen in the world. You never can tell. Maybe I'll tumble downstairs and marry a princess too," thought the fir tree, who believed every word of the story because such a nice man had told it.

The tree looked forward to the following day, when they would deck it again with fruit and toys, candles and gold. "Tomorrow I shall not quiver," it decided. "I'll enjoy my splendour to the full. Tomorrow I shall hear about Humpty-Dumpty again, and perhaps about Ivedy-Avedy too." All night long the tree stood silent as it dreamed its dreams, and next morning the butler and the maid came in with their dusters.

"Now my splendour will be renewed," the fir tree thought. But they dragged it upstairs to the garret, and there they left it in a dark corner where no daylight ever came. "What's the meaning of this?" the tree wondered.

"What am I going to do here? What stories shall I hear?" It leaned against the wall, lost in dreams. It had plenty of time for dreaming, as the days and the nights went by. Nobody came to the garret. And when at last someone did come, it was only to put many big boxes away in the corner. The tree was quite hidden. One might think it had been entirely forgotten.

"It's still winter outside," the tree thought. "The earth is too hard and covered with snow for them to plant me now. I must have been put here for shelter until springtime comes. How thoughtful of them! How good people are! Only, I wish it weren't so dark here, and so very, very lonely. There's not even a little hare. It was so friendly out in the woods when the snow was on the ground and the hare came hopping along. Yes, he was friendly even when he jumped right over me, though I did not think so then. Here it's all so terribly lonely."

"Squeak, squeak!" said a little mouse just then. He scurried across the floor, and another one followed him. They sniffed the fir tree, and rustled in and out among its branches.

"It is fearfully cold," one of them said. "Except for that, it would be very nice here, wouldn't it, you old fir tree?"

"I'm not at all old," said the fir tree. "Many trees are much older than I am."

"Where did you come from?" the mice asked him. "And what do you know?" They were most inquisitive creatures.

"Tell us about the most beautiful place in the world. Have you been there? Were you ever in the larder, where there are cheeses on shelves and hams that hang from the rafters? It's the place where you can dance upon tallow candles – where you can dart in thin and squeeze out fat."

"I know nothing of that place," said the tree. "But I know the woods where the sun shines and the little birds sing."

Then it told them about its youth. The little mice had never heard the like of it. They listened very intently, and said, "My! How much you have seen! And how happy it must have made you."

"I?" The fir tree thought about it. "Yes, those days were rather amusing." And he went on to tell them about Christmas Eve, when it was decked out with sweets and candles.

"Oh," said the little mice, "how lucky you have been, you old fir tree!"

"I am not at all old," it insisted. "I came out of the woods just this winter, and I'm really in the prime of life, though at the moment my growth is suspended."

"How nicely you tell things," said the mice. The next night they came with four other mice to hear what the tree had to say. The more it talked, the more clearly it recalled things, and it thought, "Those were happy times. But they may still come back – they may come back again. Humpty-Dumpty fell downstairs, and yet he married the Princess. Maybe the same thing will happen to me." It thought about a charming little birch tree that grew out in the woods. To the fir tree she was a real and lovely Princess.

"Who is Humpty-Dumpty?" the mice asked it. So the fir tree told them the whole story, for it could remember it word by word. The little mice were ready to jump to the top of the tree for joy. The next night many more mice came to see the fir tree, and on Sunday two rats paid it a call, but they said that the story was not very amusing. This made the little mice so sad that they began to find it not so very interesting either.

"Is that the only story you know?" the rats asked.

"Only that one," the tree answered. "I heard it on the happiest evening of my life, but I did not know then how happy I was."

"It's a very silly story. Don't you know one that tells about bacon and candles? Can't you tell us a good larder story?"

"No," said the tree.

"Then good-bye, and we won't be back," the rats said, and went away.

At last the little mice took to staying away too. The tree sighed, "Oh, wasn't it pleasant when those gay little mice sat around and listened to all that I had to say. Now that, too, is past and gone. But I will take good care to enjoy myself, once they let me out of here."

When would that be? Well, it came to pass on a morning when people came up to clean out the garret. The boxes were moved, the tree was pulled out and thrown – thrown hard – on the floor. But a servant dragged it at once to the stairway, where there was daylight again.

"Now my life will start all over," the tree thought. It felt the fresh air and the first sunbeam strike it as it came out into the courtyard. This all happened so quickly and there was so much going on around it, that the tree forgot to give even a glance at itself. The courtyard adjoined a garden, where flowers were blooming. Great masses of fragrant roses hung over the picket fence. The lime trees were in blossom, and between them the swallows skimmed past, calling, "Tilira-lira-lee, my love's come back to me." But it was not the fir tree of whom they spoke.

"Now I shall live again," it rejoiced, and tried to stretch out its branches. Alas, they were withered, and brown, and brittle. It was tossed into a corner, among weeds and nettles. But the gold star that was still tied to its top sparkled bravely in the sunlight.

Several of the merry children, who had danced around the tree and taken such pleasure in it at Christmas, were playing in the courtyard. One of the youngest seized upon it and tore off the tinsel star.

"Look what is still hanging on that ugly old Christmas tree," the child said, and stamped upon the branches until they cracked beneath his shoes.

The tree saw the beautiful flowers blooming freshly in the garden. It saw itself, and wished that they had left it in the darkest corner of the garret. It thought of its own young days in the deep woods, and of the merry Christmas Eve, and of the little mice who bad been so pleased when it told them the story of Humpty-Dumpty.

"My days are over and past," said the poor tree. "Why didn't I enjoy them while I could? Now they are gone – all gone."

A servant came and chopped the tree into little pieces. These heaped together quite high. The wood blazed beautifully under the big copper kettle, and the fir tree moaned so deeply that each groan sounded like a muffled shot. That's why the children who were playing near-by ran to make a circle around the flames, staring into the fire and crying, "Pif! Paf!" But as each groan burst from it, the tree thought of a bright summer day in the woods, or a starlit winter night. It thought of Christmas Eve and thought of Humpty-Dumpty, which was the only story it ever heard and knew how to tell. And so the tree was burned completely away.

The children played on in the courtyard. The youngest child wore on his chest the gold star that had topped the tree on its happiest night of all. But that was no more, and the tree was no more, and there's no more to my story. No more, nothing more. All stories come to an end.